BACK FROM THE BRINK OF
_____!!

Annette L. Austin

Back from the Brink of _____!!
Copyright © 2023 by Annette L. Austin

Printed in the United States of America

ISBN: 979-8-218-12344-4 (paperback)

Published by: Joseph's Ministry, LLC
www.josephsministryllc.com

Cover Illustration
by Delaney Kiah Patton

Table of Contents

DEDICATION

I wish to dedicate this book to my best friend of over twenty years, Veronica (Roni) Lynn Covington. Thank you for listening to me, crying with me, praying for me and with me, and supporting me in this journey of getting this out. I miss you daily. I thank God for placing you in my life and for the times we spent together. I will never forget you nor our unending friendship. I love you.

REVIEW

THIS IS PHENOMENAL! I am godly proud of your strength, your candor, your transparency, and so much more...

I may have known you in prior years as others have, but you explaining you here leaves no excuse for misunderstanding ANYthing. I'm sitting here with sweaty eyeballs, REALLY wanting to read it again, and again. My heart aches, my soul rejoices, my imagination soars, my arms wanna squeeze you, and my empathy heightens. I love you. THIS BOOK only escalated that love.

Dr. Mrs. Rose Perry, D-Min Biblical Counseling, Singer, Songwriter, Gospel Music Director
Fayetteville, NC

INTRODUCTION

When I was going through my crisis of faith in 2007 (how I refer to a rough period in my mid-thirties) and was in a deep depression, I needed something to bring relief but didn't know what that would be.

I had just come through a medical procedure and was home recovering. I was having nightmares while taking the pain medication I was given. I wanted the medication to numb the pain, but it didn't. God has often times used books to speak directly to me.

I went in search of a book that would fit my condition/situation. Something that could help me sort through what I was feeling and experiencing. I felt adrift, lost, and alone. I wanted to hear from an African-American author who had experienced what I had and came out on the other side with mind and soul intact.

I could not locate such a resource. I searched the world wide web and came up empty. Thus, this memoir is what I wish I'd had in hand to read, and help me to grieve, process, and even encourage me during that season of my life.

CHAPTER 1: BACK FROM THE BRINK OF

<u>DISAPPOINTMENT</u>

For my life, I had vision.

How I thought things would go.

Didn't give much thought to obstacles.

But time after time, difficulty came.

Menstrual cycle. Cramps. Pain and discomfort.

Month and month. Year after year.

Doctor Visits. No Answers. Continued Prayers.

Wondering. Contemplating. Thinking. Overanalyzing.

Vicious Cycle.

I found an African American OBGYN.

I thought it might be better.

It was not. It was torturous.

Same questionnaire. Same answers. No pregnancy.

No support. Parenting magazines. Rude nurses.

Yearly pap smears. Within normal limits.

I always said GOD is comical.

He has a sense of humor.

Ha—too many times to mention.

He would have me, Annette LaShaune

Befriend single mothers or pregnant ladies.

They always became special to me.

Not that I craved their friendship.

But God would soften my heart,

And my resolve. To support them.

No matter where I was—emotionally.

Various seasons intensified my emotional pain.

God, why not me? No, seriously?

Kept Hope. Found a Friend. Miriam.

Shared her story. Similar to mine.

We both felt like the minority.

And unfortunately, we were. Twice over.

Endometriosis stole her chance for motherhood.

People would say: Pray!! Have Faith!!

I threw baby showers for others.

I bought "boy clothes" in faith.

Kept on living. Built a house.

Two rooms specifically with blue carpet.

Still remaining in faith. Believing God.

Further research. Courage increased. Tried ICSI (see appendix for further explanation).

Procedure Expensive and extensive. Emotionally exhausting.

Shots and ultrasounds. Ultrasounds and shots.

Three weeks away from home. Alone.

God, what am I doing here?

Stay focused. Stay positive. Stay hopeful.

Overstimulated in producing eggs. Hormones erratic.

Extracted four eggs. Joined with sperm.

Wait and watch. Watch and wait.

Re-insert into the womb. Back home.

Wait and see if it worked.

No guarantees. No refunds. No Plan-B.

HCG (see appendix for further explanation) tells the story. Levels fluctuate.

Waiting for a positive pregnancy test.

We are pregnant. Shocked and speechless.

Progressed to five weeks—then miscarried.

Shocked. Speechless. Sad. Sat in silence.

Spent three weeks existing, not living.

Going through the motions. Still silent.

Friends came. Meals came. Flowers came.

Nightmares came. Anger came. Tears came.

I didn't want to hear scriptures,

About Hannah, Sarah, Elizabeth, nor Rachel.

When I felt more like Naomi.

Where was GOD? He was there.

Three weeks passed. Had a D&C (see appendix for further explanation).

Can a person get beyond disappointment?

The answer to the question: YES!

Disappointment: Can be defined as being...

Unsettled by a GOD-GIVEN appointment (circa M.B. 1997-1998).

Selah: Pause; calmly think on that.

WHAT NEXT?

How I reconciled/handled my disappointment?

    a. Realized "I mustn't be childish (i.e., throw a tantrum, pout, silent treatment), BUT CHILDLIKE."

    b. Who dealt with disappointment in scripture?

        i. Sarah, Hannah, Naomi, Moses, Joseph, Paul.

    c. Matured in my walk with Christ.

Write down any initial thoughts that come to mind at this moment.

_____

_____

_____

_____

_____

_____

CHAPTER 2: BACK FROM THE BRINK OF DISCONNECTION

I thought I knew some people.

I thought some people knew me.

Then something happened. I was alone.

I lost twins. I lost friends.

They heard words. Not my heart.

They heard me but didn't listen.

The same thing happened to JOB.

His cohorts listened but didn't hear.

I needed something they couldn't give.

People I had known for years.

Could not relate to my sorrow.

Who could get me? Feel me?

Alone in my grief. Pain. Disillusionment.

What we had before? Now wasn't.

All the church colloquialisms were said.

None stopped tears. None brought relief.

They gave sympathy. I needed empathy.

People would ask, what about adoption?

It's like comparing apples to oranges.

Please do not ask that question.

It's not helpful in any manner.

There is no substitute. No replacement.

You really think I didn't try?

We did. Attended foster care training.

Weekly trainings. Home inspection. Submitted paperwork.

Application done. Fingerprints taken. Background check.

Procedures were followed. End result. Zero.

Even considered therapeutic fostering. Didn't work.

I sought counsel. Supposedly a Christian.

One session. She offered no advice.

Could barely digest what I said.

Like it was all a dream.

I needed help. I was drowning.

Desperate for someone to get it.

To get me? Can't anyone discern?

They have eyes but cannot see.

They have ears but cannot hear.

Then one day, I found "AGAPE."

Grief group for losses—all kinds.

Miscarriage. Stillbirth. SIDS. Placental Abruption. Ectopic.

WHAT A RELIEF! I WASN'T ALONE!

Group became life-changing for me.

Some ladies were women of faith.

Struggling, emotional, angry, misunderstood, fractured, vulnerable.

From all demographics. We all HURT.

In a way that's sometimes indescribable.

Our common denominator was heartfelt pain.

We listened. We wept. We grieved.

Our grief had no expiration date.

Days turned into weeks. No babies.

Weeks turned into months. No babies.

Holidays came. Anniversaries went. No babies.

Church Christenings. Babysitting. Kids' birthday parties.

I would force myself to go.

Just to save face. I sank.

Didn't give myself grace—to escape.

Learned many lessons during that season.

Several months later. At my house.

Gathered with two girls, Merci and Justice.

Justice, only nineteen at the time.

Dropped a prophetic word of insight.

She said to me: What if…..

This is God's way to save???

(Loss = Salvation of their very souls)

#toseekandsavethelost (Luke 19:10)

Selah, pause and think on that.

Then to me, God quietly whispered.

Are you a brat? (Spiritually Immature?)

You throwing grown-up temper tantrums?

Why are you behaving this way?

Because your experience was unsatisfactory? Really?

Because you didn't get your way?

PONDER

How I reconciled/handled my disconnection?

    a. Time does not heal all wounds.

    b. God is Jehovah Rophe-God Heals (See Exodus 15:22-26)

    c. Take it slow. Day by day.

    d. Learn your triggers. Give yourself grace.

I always remember. I don't forget.

Heavenly Angels. Adam Micah. Autumn Michelle.

Returned to Scripture. Looked at Jesus.

"Philip saith unto him, Lord, shew us the Father, and it sufficeth us. Jesus saith unto him, Have I been so long time with you, and yet hast thou not known me, Philip? he that hath seen me hath seen the Father; and how sayest thou then, Shew us the Father?"
John 14: 8-9 KJV

"All things are delivered unto me of my Father: and no man knoweth the Son, but the Father; neither knoweth any man the Father, save the Son, and he to whomsoever the Son will reveal him."
Matthew 11:27

FRIENDS BECAME STRANGERS.

STRANGERS BECAME FRIENDS.

"Can two walk together, except they be agreed?"
Amos 3:3 KJV

Write down any initial thoughts that come to mind at this moment.

_____

_____

_____

_____

CHAPTER 3: BACK FROM THE BRINK OF

<u>DEPRESSION</u>

Vision was cloudy. Couldn't see clearly.

The struggle was real in 1996.

Couldn't sleep peacefully Had no appetite.

Warped thinking. Injure yourself, then rest.

Wreck your car. Rest in hospital.

The enemy's job—steal, kill, destroy (John 10:10).

I didn't know it back then.

My eyes were darkened. No light.

I felt helpless. I felt hopeless.

I didn't wanna die, per se.

I just knew I was dismal.

Sadder than I'd ever been before.

Didn't know why. Constantly stressed out.

Discontent. Unsettled. Nothing right. Everything wrong.

Feeling the weight of the world.

It was on October 31, 1996.

Halloween night. Became my breaking point.

Husband drove me to the hospital.

Cared enough to get me help.

Landstuhl Hospital. Fifth floor. Self-Admitted.

Brain foggy. Brain unsure. Brain restless.

It was a God Ordained setup.

My intake clerk. A Christian brother.

Told me point blank, straight up.

You know you don't belong here.

Huh! Scuse me? Say what now?

He didn't know me from Adam (figure of speech).

He began speaking life. Even then.

Zoloft. Individual therapy. Group therapy. Sleep.

After seven days, back to work.

Something in me had changed. Shifted.

The spirit of heaviness began lifting.

First time. In a long time.

I felt like I could breathe.

Depression is a brain's chemical imbalance.

I got the help I needed.

Thus, began my spiritual awakening. LIFE.

There was another instance, I recalled.

The Lord gave me this scripture.

I didn't know it was BIBLE.

I was a babe in Christ.

At the time. Learning to listen.

Learning to worship. Learning to pray.

The Lord said to me—Annette,

fruit of your womb is blessed.

I had no point of reference:

No understanding, of what that could mean.

This was approximately June of 1998.

I couldn't imagine what would transpire.

Then in 2012, around March timeframe.

The Lord spoke to me again.

"I did not lie to you."

He whispered into my broken heart.

From God's lips to my ears.

I realized that was the truth.

The Lord gave Jesus—for me.

According to John 3:16. Scripture helped.

So that day, I gained peace.

His unexplainable peace. His calm presence.

I could not argue with facts.

How I reconciled/handled my depression?

    a. Realized I was beyond helping myself.

    b. Keep asking for the help you need.

    c. Meds, therapy, Jesus—all work in tandem.

    d. Get to a place of surrender.

Write down any initial thoughts that come to mind at this moment.

_____

_____

_____

_____

CHAPTER 4: BACK FROM THE BRINK OF

DESTRUCTION

A global pandemic bent on destruction.

Spread like wildfire—across the globe.

A president, not for the people.

Black bodies slain because of fear.

People fear what they don't understand.

Low, Medium, High levels of anxiety.

Low, Medium, High levels of depression.

Where is God? Does He see?

See our land. Desolate. In despair.

Wickedness in the land. Sin rampant.

How can we rebound from this?

Pestilence, Death, Sorrow. Vaccinations = Band Aid

Examine the root of the problem.

It always goes back to sin.

Too much faith in a system.

Too much faith in a man.

The antidote for sin is LOVE (John 3:16).

For God so loved the world

He gave his only begotten son

That whosoever believeth in him shall

Not perish but have everlasting life.

I, too, lost family to COVID-19.

An uncle in a nursing home.

No family allowed. Died all alone.

He was a Christian and veteran.

Many battles. Some won. Some lost.

Just heartbreaking for friends and family.

Nobody was left unaffected or impacted.

Rampant minority maltreatment. Modern-day lynchings.

Black bodies slain in the streets.

Mothers and fathers crying over sheets.

Seen as threats, not as PEOPLE.

Why aren't they seen as redeemable?

Time after time. Again and again.

How and will it ever end?

Timelines cut short. Families left behind.

Burying loved ones. Time after time.

Sons without Fathers. Daughters without Dads.

A vicious cycle. Making us mad.

Black Lives Matter. God's Image Bearers.

Why show hate based on race?

Stop showing HATE TO OUR RACE!

Love covers a multitude of sins.

Forgiveness and empathy shall ultimately win.

Bitterness kills from the inside out.

Justice is what we demand NOW!

Differences don't have to divide us.

You can choose to be different.

Know your history, do not repeat.

I took a trip to Whitney.

Whitney Plantation located near Kenner, Louisiana.

In 2021, with a caucasian woman.

From Massachusetts. Her name is Shania.

Rode through Arkansas, Mississippi, and Louisiana.

Ten hours filled with nervous energy.

To experience the grounds. Walk around.

It was heart-stopping, gut-wrenching,

And terrifyingly mysterious all at once.

My mind and emotions were racing.

To look. To listen. To digest.

How I analyzed this climate's destruction?

    a. Pray for rain. Pray for change.

    b. YOU—don't let hate beget hate.

    c. For your own sanity, LET GO (of the evil that besets us)!

    d. By faith, make a different choice.

Jesus' words and actions drew people.

Draw from your ancestors' unequaled resilience.

You don't have to stay angry.

Use your anger as a catalyst.

You...do what you can do.

In your sphere of influence TODAY!

Write down any initial thoughts that come to mind at this moment.

_____

_____

_____

_____

_____

_____

_____

_____

_____

_____

CHAPTER 5: BACK FROM THE BRINK OF

DESIRE

The ache never completely goes away.

I saw myself with a man-child.

Him and me. Me and him.

I never imagined myself without him.

I'm not sure when it started.

I don't know if it'll end.

When I see moms and sons.

My heart feels some kinda way.

Curious sometimes. Sad sometimes. Jealous sometimes.

Seeing adult sons—caring for moms.

My heart aches in a way.

What would my son be like?

How would he see the world?

It is normal to have desire.

Being a godparent fills the hole.

Serving someone's son fills the hole.

Mentor. Advise. Listen. Share. Encourage. Aspire.

A cousin. A nephew. A brother.

Show empathy. Be kind. Pray. Comfort.

These are all ways to contribute.

All is not lost. Use desire.

Use it to sow some seeds.

This chapter honors my surrogate sons.

I smile. I cry. I remember.

All is not lost. Paths Crossed.

No regrets. No regrets. No regrets.

I did what I could do.

How I reconciled my natural desire?

    a. Use the desire inside of you.

    b. Don't let desire go to waste.

    c. Ask God to help you put things into proper perspective concerning your life (not focusing on others).

Write down any initial thoughts that come to mind at this moment.

_____

_____

_____

_____

_____

_____

_____

_____

_____

CHAPTER 6: BACK FROM THE BRINK OF

DEATH

Loss is hard. Many tears fall.

Hearts are broken. Dreams are shattered.

We never forget. We always remember.

Loss touches everyone around the globe.

It is just one common denominator.

Thank God for what connects us.

We are more alike than different.

Human beings. We feel. We hurt.

Kendy from Philippines still grieving loss.

Annette from OK struggles with failure.

Sienna of NC misses eldest daily.

Marshell of PA visits tiny grave.

Death in any form is difficult.

The end of something or someone.

Life is hard. Hills and valleys.

Ups and downs. Ebbs and flows.

Death can cause mental anguish/breakdown.

We act irrationally. We act hastily.

We make errors in judgment unintentionally.

We are flawed. We get desperate,

For relief from weight and pressure.

We need help. We need rescuing.

Oftentimes, it's hard to accurately articulate.

What's going on? What's going wrong?

Car accident. Had more than one.

Life flashed before my eyes. Blank.

I never saw it coming. Shock.

Ambulance. Paramedics. Gurney. Neck brace. Sirens.

Hospital. Non-life-threatening injuries. Scary.

Heart beating fast. Could've been gone.

GOD SAID NO! Daughter, LIVE ON!

Paused and pondered. Wondered and worried.

Searched for the lesson. The "WHY?"

Bad things happen to good people.

Some questions do not have answers.

Had to learn to accept it.

Live on without filling the blanks.

It's not easy, but it's doable.

You have to want to live.

Sometimes I didn't. Sometimes I did.

How I adapted and accepted death?

    a. Ask myself, "What kind of legacy will you leave?"

        i. Help someone.

        ii. Bless someone.

        iii. Speak kindly to someone.

        iv. Believe in someone.

        v. Restore someone.

        vi. Support someone.

        vii. Invest in someone.

        viii. Encourage someone.

    b. How will your life matter?

    c. How will your life count?

    d. How will you contribute?

    e. What/who will you build?

    f. What/who will outlast you?

g. What mark will you make?

h. What does your life presently say?

Write down any initial thoughts that come to mind at this moment.

_____

_____

_____

_____

_____

_____

_____

ABOUT THE AUTHOR

Annette L Austin holds a Bachelor of Science in Accounting from the University of North Carolina-Fayetteville State University, as well as an undergrad degree in Biblical Studies and a Master's in Divinity from the Family Bible College of Fayetteville, NC. She spent almost eight years as a Traffic Management Coordinator for the United States Army. She has served her community as a volunteer in multiple non-profit organizations, including a grief group in Fayetteville, NC called A.G.A.P.E., as well as a mission volunteer with Asking for the Nations in Sand Springs, Oklahoma. She has a heart for special needs students, is a strong advocate for education, and lives by the motto, there is life beyond infertility. She resides in Broken Arrow, Oklahoma, with her husband of twenty-eight years and her beloved dog, Sebastian.

APPENDIX

ICSI – Intracytoplasmic Sperm Injection

Before a man's sperm can fertilize a woman's egg, the head of the sperm must attach to the outside. Once attached, the sperm pushes through the outer layer to the inside of the egg (cytoplasm), where fertilization occurs.

Sometimes the sperm cannot penetrate the outer layer for various reasons. The egg's outer layer may be thick or hard to penetrate, or the sperm may be unable to swim. In these cases, an intracytoplasmic sperm injection (ICSI) can be done along with in vitro fertilization (IVF) to help fertilize the egg. During ICSI, a single sperm is injected directly into the egg's cytoplasm.

There are two ways that an egg may be fertilized by IVF: traditional and ICSI. In traditional IVF, 50,000 or more swimming sperm are placed next to the egg in a laboratory dish. Fertilization occurs when one of the sperm enters the cytoplasm of the egg. In the ICSI process, a tiny needle, called a micropipette, is used to inject a single sperm into the center of the egg. With either traditional IVF or ICSI, once fertilization occurs, the fertilized egg (now called an embryo) grows in a laboratory for one to five days before it is transferred to the woman's uterus (womb).

Source: https://www.reproductivefacts.org/news-and-publications/patient-fact-sheets-and-booklets/documents/fact-sheets-and-info-booklets/what-is-intracytoplasmic-sperm-injection-icsi/

HCG – Human Chorionic Gonadotropin

An HCG pregnancy test checks human chorionic gonadotropin (HCG) levels in the blood or urine. This measurement means that an HCG test can determine whether a person is pregnant and whether their body is producing the right level of pregnancy hormones. Also called a beta HCG test, this blood test measures the specific HCG hormone in your blood in international units per liter (IU/L). The level of HCG helps determine the age of the fetus. HCG levels rise in the first trimester and then drop slightly. They typically peak at 28,000–210,000 IU/L around twelve weeks after conception.

Source: https://www.medicalnewstoday.com/articles/327284

D & C – Dilation and Curettage

Dilation and curettage (D&C) is a procedure to remove tissue from inside your uterus. Health care providers perform dilation and curettage to diagnose and treat certain uterine conditions — such as heavy bleeding — or to clear the uterine lining after a miscarriage or abortion.

In a dilation and curettage, your provider uses small instruments or a medication to open (dilate) the lower, narrow part of your uterus (cervix). Your provider then uses a surgical instrument called a curette, which can be a sharp instrument or suction device, to remove uterine tissue.

Source: https://www.mayoclinic.org/tests-procedures/dilation-and-curettage/about/pac-20384910

CPSIA information can be obtained
at www.ICGtesting.com
Printed in the USA
JSHW020430250223
38184JS00003B/141